HAMSTERS,
GERBILS,
GUINEA PIGS,
PET MICE,
AND PET RATS

HAMSTERS GERBILS GUINEA PIGS PET MICE & PET RATS

BY JAMES AND LYNN HAHN

 A FIRST BOOK

FRANKLIN WATTS | NEW YORK | LONDON | 1977

TO PAPA
who taught us to love, respect,
and treat all animals
with kindness and affection

Library of Congress Cataloging in Publication Data

Hahn, James.
    Hamsters, gerbils, guinea pigs, pet mice, and
pet rats.

    (A First book)
    Includes index.
    SUMMARY: General information on the history
of these rodents and instructions for raising them
as pets.
    1. Rodents as pets—Juvenile literature. [1.
Rodents as pets. 2. Pets] I. Hahn, Lynn, joint
author. II. Title.
SF459.R63H33   636'.93'23   77–1389
ISBN 0–531–01287–5

10

CONTENTS

HAMSTERS,
GERBILS,
GUINEA PIGS,
PET MICE,
AND PET RATS

LIVING DOWN A BAD NAME

When you mention the word rodent, a lot of people wrinkle their noses in disgust. They immediately think of wild rats and mice as carriers of filth and disease. They probably don't know that the rodent family tree has over 2,000 branches, including the squirrel, the chipmunk, and our friends the gerbil, the guinea pig, and the hamster.

The rat got its bad name many centuries ago. Rats often raided garbage near homes. When cities began building sewer systems, starting with the ancient Romans, rats were given a convenient, sheltered place to live and breed. During the 1300s, people all over Europe feared and hated rats, because they spread the bubonic plague, a disease that killed millions. The tame rats raised today are related to these disease-carriers. But pet rats are now no more like wild rats than dogs are like their wild relatives, wolves.

For many centuries, mice were generally felt to be as big a pest as rats. Our word for mouse actually comes from an ancient Sanskrit word meaning "thief." Field mice ravaged crops, house mice stole food and contaminated food and water supplies, and a mousetrap became a necessity in every household.

Many cultures believed that seeing a mouse was a sign of bad things to come. For example, if a mouse gnawed at your clothes or you dreamt of a mouse, you were probably going to die soon. Ancient Jewish folklore forbade the eating of any food a mouse had chewed on, because it could cause forgetfulness, or at the least a sore throat. One story on the origin of mice claims that they were created by the devil on Noah's Ark. Another story holds that the devil himself came on board the Ark in the form of a mouse and gnawed a hole in it to make it sink.

But some ancient cultures looked on mice with more respect. In ancient Egypt, cooked mouse was used to cure a variety of ills—including stomach aches! In ancient Greece, the god Apollo was sometimes called Apollo Smintheus, meaning Apollo the Mouse. To honor him, white mice were kept in Apollo's temples under the altar. And some stories from the past actually credited mice or rats with punishing evil people. One popular legend told of the German bishop of Bingen, who hoarded all the corn in his region. The next year, there was a famine. The bishop began selling his corn to the starving peasants at prices they couldn't afford. But the peasants got their revenge. One day, rats swarmed into the bishop's barns and ate all the corn. Then they swept into the bishop's castle tower—and ate the bishop!

Above: in this drawing, the rat is made to look like a real villain. Below: But this pet rat is really gentle and clean.

Nevertheless, it took quite a long time for mice and rats to be welcomed into people's homes as pets. The first ones to appear in North America didn't come as invited guests. They came as stowaways on ships from Europe. Both laboratory studies and careful breeding have helped to make these animals more welcome. Writers and cartoonists have also contributed a great deal to changing people's attitudes toward them. In spite of their bad name, mice have often appeared as charming, timid creatures in stories, fairy tales, poems, and children's nursery rhymes. And perhaps nothing did more to endear the mouse to people all over the world than the birth, in 1928, of Walt Disney's lovable cartoon character Mickey Mouse. Mickey became famous the world over almost as soon as he was created. He became so popular, in fact, that the Allies used his name as the secret password for the D-Day invasion of France in World War II.

Thus, pet mice and rats have been slowly living down their bad names. In fact, they are fast becoming, along with hamsters, gerbils, and guinea pigs, some of today's most popular pets.

The mouse has been depicted both affectionately and comically. Above is an illustration from "Menage de Souris," or the House of Mouse, published in Germany in 1934. Below is artist Charles Folkard's conception of the "Three Blind Mice," a Mother Goose nursery rhyme.

THE GUINEA PIG: A SOUTH AMERICAN IMMIGRANT

The gentle, affectionate guinea pig doesn't look at all like a mouse or rat. People never feared it like its rodent cousins. Incas in Peru kept guinea pigs as pets and for meat several centuries ago. In the 1500s, Spanish explorers took some of the tame little creatures back to Europe. Guinea pigs were so affectionate that, for a time, they became as popular for pets as lap dogs.

How the guinea pig got its name is one of the great mysteries of the animal world. These cute little animals aren't related to pigs and don't act like pigs. But they do squeal and grunt when they're hungry. This probably explains the "pig" part of their name.

No one is exactly sure how early owners connected Guinea, the name of a country on the west coast of Africa, with these furry South American natives. Some think the animals were named for the traders who carried them to Europe. These traders were called Guineamen, because they began their trips in Guinea, sailed to South America, where they picked up the animals, then sailed to England, where they sold them.

A short-haired Bolivian *Cavia Porcellus,* or guinea pig

Some historians think the people who named the guinea pig were confused. Although guinea pigs were native to the Andes Mountains in Peru, Colombia, and Ecuador, European traders picked them up in the South American country called Dutch Guiana. Since most of the people in the 1500s weren't familiar with the name Guiana, they may have simply pronounced it like the more familiar name, Guinea. Other historians say English people of the time used the word Guinea as a general term for any unknown, distant country.

Many people who raise guinea pigs today insist on using the name *cavies,* from the full scientific name *Cavia Porcellus*. But whatever you call them, these lovable animals have provided people with enjoyment for hundreds of years.

HAMSTERS AND GERBILS: SOME LATECOMERS TO THE PET WORLD

Newspapers and books published in the 1800s reported that hamsters lived in the Middle East and "gerbilles" in Northern India. But at the time, no one seemed interested in these animals. Wild hamsters in Europe had already earned the contempt of European farmers. An English natural history book published in 1849 said the English were lucky not to have them in their country. These larger relatives of today's pet hamsters stole huge amounts of grain from farmers' fields and stored it in their burrows. The hamsters didn't eat all the grain, they just liked to store it! This behavior earned them their name, which comes from the German word *hamstern,* meaning "to hoard."

But in the 1930s both hamsters and gerbils became important to people. In 1930, Professor I. Aharoni, a scientist at the Hebrew University in Jerusalem, found a mother golden hamster and her twelve babies in their burrow in the Syrian desert. Thinking they would be useful for research, the professor carried ten of the baby hamsters back to his laboratory. During the trip, all but three

died or escaped. Four months later, one of the females produced the first litter of captive hamsters.

At first it was thought that hamsters were nervous and bad-tempered. But they were kept anyway, since they were useful for scientific experiments. The hamsters multiplied rapidly and some were shipped abroad. Eventually, researchers discovered that if hamsters were handled gently, they would become tame and friendly. Many lab workers took them home. Before long, many people were enjoying these furry little animals as pets.

Gerbils also came to the pet world by way of the laboratory. The Experimental Animals Research Committee in Japan was looking for a rodent to use in studying human diseases. They thought the gerbils living in Eastern Mongolia would be perfect. So, in 1935, the committee imported twenty pairs of them.

In 1954, Dr. Victor Schwentker, a genetics researcher from New York, had sent to him eleven pairs of these gerbils' descendants. The gerbil's friendly, good-natured, curious personality quickly captivated pet lovers everywhere. All the pet gerbils in the United States today are descendants of the ones sent to Dr. Schwentker in 1954.

Above: a family of golden hamsters
Below: a Mongolian gerbil, quietly taking in the sights and sounds of his natural home, the desert. You can always quickly tell a gerbil from a hamster by its tail.

LAB ASSISTANTS

Hamsters, gerbils, mice, rats, and guinea pigs are some of our most valuable assistants in battling disease and in learning how our bodies and minds work. Almost 2,000 years ago, the Roman writer Pliny recommended mouse ashes mixed with honey to cure earaches. Cooked mice were once used to treat whooping cough, smallpox, measles, and many other ailments. Even today, some people still believe that fried mice or mouse pie is a cure for bed-wetting.

Today, rodents help us in much more scientific ways. In fact, as we have seen, hamsters, gerbils, mice, and rats were used in laboratories before anyone kept them as pets. Guinea pigs were pets before they became lab helpers. But they have helped scientists in so many experiments that the term guinea pig now refers to anyone who is the subject of an experiment.

Rodents make ideal laboratory animals because they're small, they don't eat much, they reproduce quickly, and they react very much like people do to drugs, changes in diet, and many other scientific tests.

Disease | By studying rodents, scientists all over the world have learned a great deal about what causes various

A large rodent farm in upstate New York. The rats raised here
are sent to laboratories all over. Notice the charts on the cages.
Careful records of age, weight, diet, and so on, are kept on each animal.

diseases and how to prevent them. Japanese scientists first used gerbils, whose scientific name is *Meriones unguiculatus,* to study leprosy and rabies, among other diseases. Studies with guinea pigs have helped scientists learn about tuberculosis, diphtheria, and cancer. Mice have also been used in cancer research. Today, rats are helping environmental scientists discover how air, water, land, and noise pollution affect our bodies and our minds.

Drugs | Many drugs, such as aspirin and penicillin, were first tested on rodents before they were used on people. Guinea pigs are especially useful for testing anti-allergy drugs. Many common skin lotions and ointments used by people today were first tested on guinea pigs, because their skin is very similar to human skin.

Surgery | Scientists have discovered that at very cool temperatures, golden hamsters, known scientifically as *Mesocricetus auratus,* go into hibernation. In hibernation, all body processes are slowed down. Doctors are studying hamster hibernation closely, to get ideas on how to lower human body temperature during surgery.

Experimenters have also discovered that the skin from other animals can be easily transplanted onto a hamster's cheek pouch. Most animals naturally reject tissues transplanted from other animals. Doctors hope that studying the hamster's cheek skin will enable them to develop better ways of transplanting human tissues and organs.

Diet and Health | Early in the 1900s, scientists began using laboratory rats to find out what vitamins and minerals animals and people need to stay healthy. They knew that rats' bodies react like human bodies when they don't receive enough of certain vitamins and minerals.

Guinea pigs have given scientists important information about how much vitamin C our bodies need. Most mammals, including other rodents, manufacture vitamin C in their bodies. But guinea pigs, like people, don't. They have to get it from their diets. When scientists didn't feed their guinea pigs foods containing vitamin C, the animals got sick. Their bodies didn't grow correctly, their gums started to bleed, and their wounds wouldn't heal properly. These are the same symptoms people have when they get scurvy, a disease we now know is caused by a lack of vitamin C.

Gerbils have helped us learn how unbalanced diets can lead to heart disease. Gerbils that eat too much fatty food, such as cheese, suffer more strokes and heart attacks. Scientists think this may be a clue to why people have strokes and heart attacks.

Heredity | Because our furry little friends can have so many children in a very short time, they are excellent subjects for studying how parents pass on traits. A pair of mice, for example, can have 135 children in twelve months. During that time their children can have children, so the number of laboratory subjects grows and grows. Scientists can study the heredity patterns of several generations of mice, rats, guinea pigs, gerbils, and hamsters in only a few years. It would take hundreds of years to study as many generations of people.

In the 1800s, European scientists began using mice to study how animals inherit hair color. Other heredity studies since have helped us understand how animals and humans pass on such traits as eye color and straightness or curliness of hair. Most of the varieties of guinea pigs, hamsters, rats, and mice developed as a result of such tests. Since laboratory workers haven't yet done much genetic experimenting with them, gerbils still come in only one coat color. Researchers also use rodents to study and understand how hereditary defects, such as diabetes, hemophilia, and color blindness, are passed from parents to children.

In Space | Scientists have used rats and mice to test how animals react to the conditions of outer space. Before people were ever sent up in rockets, rodents rode in them to make sure everything was A OK. Rodents were also used to test special machines on earth that help scientists predict how people would react to gravity changes and other conditions in outer space. We can thank our little rodent friends for helping us get safely to the moon and back.

Understanding Ourselves | Rats, mice, gerbils, and hamsters help us find out how people learn and react. Some rodents do better in certain intelligence tests than others. For example, when a rat is put into a maze with food at one end, it quickly learns how to find the food. But a gerbil is so curious it doesn't care about the food. It would rather explore every inch of the maze.

Most gerbils don't overdo their curiosity, however.

They can remember to avoid unpleasant situations, such as electrical shocks, about ten times faster than rats. In such memory research, hamsters have also been especially useful to psychologists.

Guinea pigs flunk most intelligence tests because they aren't as active and curious as other rodents. But they will sit quietly and listen to music. Psychologists have found that young children will also sit quietly and listen to the same music the guinea pigs enjoy.

Rodents also help us learn about our emotional needs. Like us, those that are given a lot of attention and affection stay healthier than those that are fed balanced diets but not given any special attention. Some research centers have successfully used gerbils to work with children who have emotional problems. Gerbils are so affectionate that they help these children learn to be friendly and loving.

SOME FASCINATING CHARACTERISTICS

Animal Athletes | Did you know that gerbils, mice, and rats have tails that are as long as their bodies? These rodents are excellent climbers and jumpers, thanks to their well-developed tails, which they use for balance. Rats and mice have scales on their tails. When they move their bodies forward, the scales on their tails lie flat against the skin. But if they move backwards, the scales pop up. This helps them grip the surface on which they are climbing.

Gerbils also have long, strong rear legs that make jumping, leaping, and running easy for them. Rats and mice have strong legs also. Mice are great gymnasts. We have spent many enjoyable hours watching them in action, leaping and climbing easily and gracefully. They can even hang upside down, clinging to things with their feet.

Maybe you and your friends will want to set up a track, some ladders, or a trapeze to see which of your pets is the best gymnast, jumper, or runner.

Senses | Rats, mice, guinea pigs, and hamsters have very bad eyes. They see best in dim night light. But their

The mouse's tail is as long as its body.

other senses are excellent. Most rodents don't recognize each other on sight. Instead, they smell, squeak, or touch each other.

Rodents' hearing is especially sensitive. They communicate with each other by making very high-pitched sounds, some of which only other rodents can hear.

Whiskers | Rodent whiskers aren't just for show. They work as sensing tools. With their whiskers they can sense smooth and rough surfaces, temperature changes, and breezes.

Teeth | All rodents have front teeth that never stop growing! A rat's teeth, for example, can grow as much as five inches a year if it doesn't have something to gnaw on. So if you have a rodent pet, be sure to give it something to gnaw on, such as hardwood, hard-shelled nuts, tree twigs, or wooden clothespins. If rodents don't keep their teeth filed down, they will have trouble eating. Their teeth could eventually grow through their mouths or into their brains, causing serious injury or even death.

Do You Stuff Your Cheeks Full of Food? | If you do, you're behaving like a hamster, which has expandable pouches in its mouth that extend down into its throat and shoulders. Hamsters love to stuff their pouches. Then they empty them by leaning forward and pushing on the pouches with their forepaws.

See how its tail helps the mouse climb and keep its balance?

Warning! | The United States Department of Agriculture has issued the following statement: BREEDERS OF HAMSTERS ARE CAUTIONED TO PREVENT THE ESCAPE OF ANY OF THESE ANIMALS. SUCH RELEASE UNDER FAVORABLE CONDITIONS MIGHT ESTABLISH THE HAMSTER IN THE WILD AND THEREBY CREATE A SERIOUS RODENT PROBLEM, SINCE THEY ARE DESTRUCTIVE TO GROWING CROPS, GARDENS, AND AGRICULTURAL ENTERPRISES. PURCHASERS SHOULD BE AWARE OF THE DANGER OF ESCAPES, AND MAKE EVERY EFFORT TO PREVENT THE ESTABLISHMENT OF A WILD COLONY. Escaped gerbils could cause similar problems. Therefore, laws in California and New Mexico prohibit keeping gerbils as pets.

Private Property! Keep Out! | Gerbils like to establish property lines. They have a flat, narrow gland on the middle of their stomach that secretes oil. On females, the gland is small. But on males, it's large and orange. It's interesting to watch a male skimming along to mark his territory. You will know a gerbil is skimming when it crawls low while rubbing its stomach against a surface. This is how it secretes the oil that leaves property lines. Other gerbils smell these lines and stay away.

Hamsters love stuffing then emptying their cheek pouches. This is how they turn ordinary paper towel or other materials into bedding.

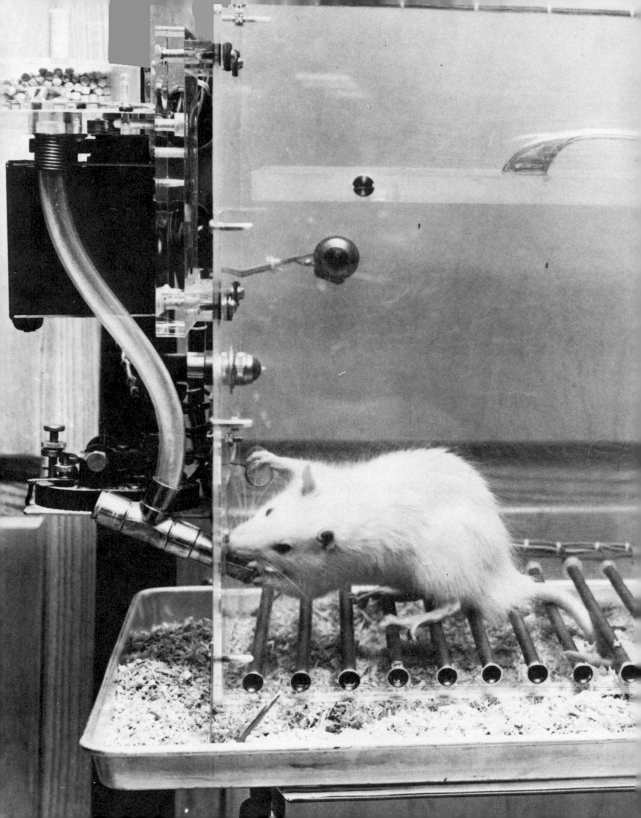

Are You a Pack Rat? | Rats have lots of fun collecting things and storing them in a pile. If you let your rat out of its home, it will bring back candy and gum wrappers, coins, rubber bands, shoelaces, pencils, keys, paper clips, and anything else it can carry away.

Hibernation | Hamsters will go into a deep sleep if the temperature inside their homes drops below 45° Fahrenheit (7° C). When they hibernate, all of their body activities, including heartbeat and breathing, slow down. Their body temperature drops, and they become stiff. They may look dead, but they aren't. A little of your body warmth and some warm milk will bring them back to normal.

Creatures of the Night | Gerbils, guinea pigs, hamsters, mice, and rats are creatures of the night, or *nocturnal* animals. They like to rest and sleep during the bright daylight hours and eat and play during the night.

Intelligence | When it comes to animal intelligence, rodents are above-average. Rats are smarter than cows, horses, and many other mammals. They learn from the past and are able to remember experiences. For example, if you aren't kind to a rat, it will remember and may not be kind to you. Rats also use logic to figure out the best way to get food. They always choose the shortest route. We're

This mouse is taking an intelligence test. Each time it gives the correct response, food drops down through the tube.

always amazed to see how quickly rats solve difficult puzzles and mazes.

Super Clean! | All the rodents we know are clean and fresh-smelling. They spend a lot of time washing and grooming their bodies, especially after eating. They moisten their forepaws in their mouths and quickly and efficiently scrub their faces—and even wash behind their ears!

SO MUCH VARIETY

A Mouse Fur Fashion Show | Did you know that pet mice are available in at least seventy different colors or color combinations? Pet mice, or fancy mice as they are sometimes called, come in colors such as black, blue, champagne, cream, dove, fawn, red, and silver. How would you like to show off an orange pet mouse, or one that's pastel-colored (the pastel undercoat is covered with a shiny, soft coat of white fur)? Maybe you would like to try breeding mice in solid colors, two-tone colors, a mixture of three colors, or a mixture of four colors. Solid-colored mice are called *selfs,* and mice with spotted coats are called *marked.*

Did you know that some mice never grow any hair at all? Some others grow long wavy hair and are called *woolies.* Still others grow long silky hair and are thus called *silkies.* And finally, some mice grow thick hair called a *rex-coat.* A curly-haired mouse with a thick coat is called *astarex.* Some astarex mice even grow whiskers that match their coats!

As Good As Gold | Do you know what kind of hamster was the first to be raised as a pet? If you said the *golden* hamster, you're right. Actually, a golden hamster has reddish-gold fur, with a grayish-white tummy, black markings on its head and cheeks, black eyes, and a wide band of dark fur across its chest.

For many years the golden hamster was the only kind of hamster people could buy. But today you can have an *albino* hamster, which has white fur and pink or red eyes, or a *cream* hamster with cream-colored fur, black eyes, and black ears. There are even *panda* hamsters, sometimes called *piebalds, spotteds,* or *harlequins,* which have golden fur and white spottings (but these are hard to tame). Some of our hamster friends have grown amber-gold or cinnamon-colored fur. Hamsters can be either short-haired or long-haired.

Only One Suit of Clothes for the Gerbil | All gerbils have light brown, black-tipped fur, with an undercoat of slate-gray. In certain places, gerbils can hide easily from their enemies because of their coloring. We bet that you couldn't spot a gerbil if it was a foot in front of you in the desert.

The Worldly Guinea Pig | Guinea pigs come in fur types and color combinations named after various countries. The *Bolivian* breed is the most common kind of guinea pig today. It has short, coarse hair that lies smoothly against its body. *Peruvian* guinea pigs, the rarest variety, look like they're hiding under a mop. They have long, silky hair that flows gently down to their feet. Our personal favorite is the *Abyssinian* guinea pig. It has short, curly, ruffled hair, which we love to run our fingers through. There is also a *Himalayan* guinea pig, which has beautiful

A long-haired Peruvian guinea pig

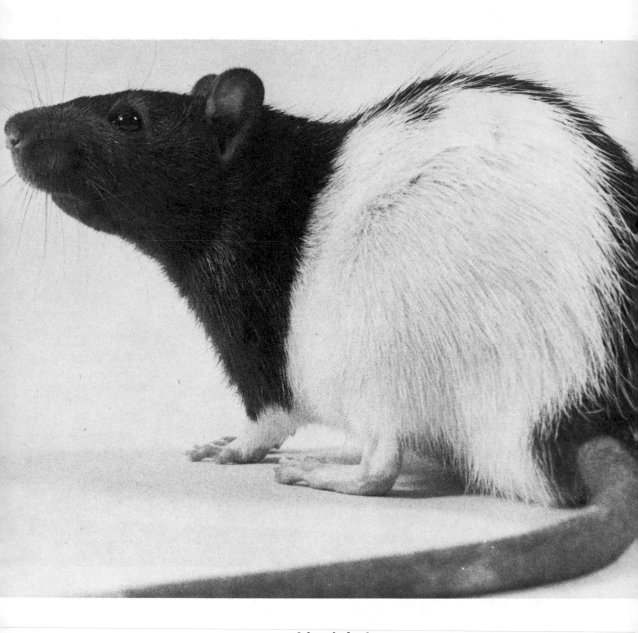

A hooded rat

white fur with little dark patches on its nose, ears, and feet. The *Dutch* variety comes with red, black, or brown hair. We have seen other guinea pigs that have white, black, tan, or orange fur, or combinations of two or three of these colors.

Rats of Different Colors | The *Irish Black* rat looks very handsome with its black coat and white markings on its feet and tail, but maybe you would like to have a *hooded* rat for a pet. Hooded rats have black or red hair on their heads and white hair on their bodies. Other kinds of pet rats include ruby-red with black eyes, brown-hooded, dark chocolate, black-eyed ivory, powder-blue, and chocolate-blue.

CHOOSING YOUR NEW RODENT PET

Take your time choosing your new rodent pet. You and your new little friend will be living together for a few years, so you should make sure you will be happy with each other. Start your looking in a clean pet store. If a store smells, looks dirty, or the animals are living in overcrowded homes, don't even think about buying a pet there. The animals will probably be sick or unfriendly.

You should also watch how the pet store workers treat the animals. We have visited some stores where the workers were so rough and unfriendly they made the animals afraid of people. You would have a hard time making friends with a mistreated animal.

Choose a Healthy Pet | Healthy rodents are alert and active. They have bright, clear, wide-open eyes. Their ears stand up straight and their fur is sleek. Don't pick a pet who has wet underparts, sores, scabs, or bald spots in its fur. Check that there are no lumps under its chin. A rodent with dull or runny eyes or a runny nose may have a cold or pneumonia. If you're choosing a gerbil, mouse, or rat, make sure its tail isn't stubby and doesn't have any bends, bumps, lumps, or kinks. Don't pick an animal that seems too fat or too thin. These are signs that the rodent has been poorly fed or has nutritional problems.

Check Its Age | Find out when the animal was born. Rodents between one and two months old will have an easier time learning to live with you. But be sure they have been weaned, which means they don't depend on their mother's milk anymore. You should also be aware that rodents who haven't grown up together may fight if you put them in the same home.

Personality Test | When you see an animal you think you would like to buy, ask the pet store worker to put it on the counter top. A healthy, happy hamster, gerbil, mouse, or rat will sniff and explore the new area. Guinea pigs don't move around as much. But a healthy guinea pig will look alert and enjoy being petted.

Ask to be shown how to pick up the rodent. Let it see and smell your hands first. Move slowly so you don't frighten it. If it seems gentle and friendly in your hands, you've found a new friend. If it seems frightened or tries to bite, try again with another animal.

How Many Should I Buy? | Gerbils, guinea pigs, mice, and rats like to have company. If possible, you should buy at least two. If you don't plan to breed your pets, choose two females. Grown males sometimes fight with each other. If you can have only one pet, be sure you can spend lots of time with it. Otherwise your little friend will get lonely.

Hamsters like to live alone. If two adults are kept in the same home, they may fight and kill each other. Unless

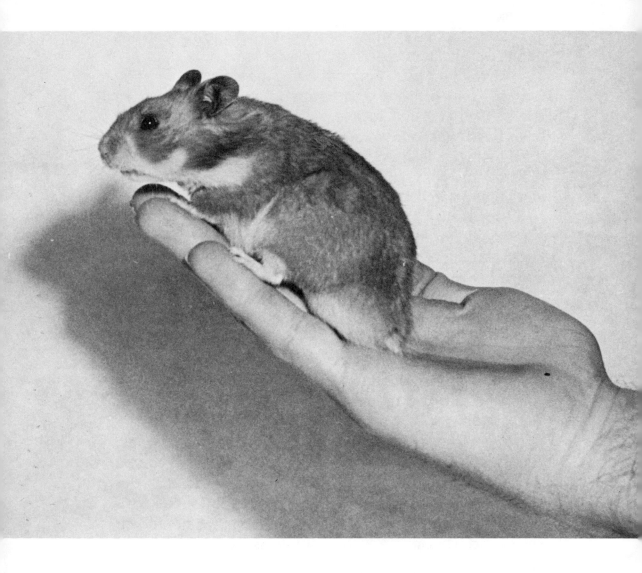

**This golden hamster sits calmly but
alertly in the pet-store owner's hand.
It will probably make a good pet.**

you're planning to breed hamsters, choose a male. Females sometimes get nervous and unfriendly as they grow older.

Don't choose rodents of different species and expect them to share a home. For example, a hamster and a rat or a rat and a mouse probably won't live together peacefully; each instinctively fears or hates the other. Guinea pigs, on the other hand, live happily with other animals.

Male or Female? | Ask the pet store worker to help you tell the males from the females. You can usually see nipples on the female's undersides. They look like two rows of small dots. You can also see the penis on male rats and mice. To find out a guinea pig's sex, gently press on its underside near the rump. If the guinea pig is a male, its penis will come out.

Female hamsters and gerbils have rounded rumps and males have longer, more narrow rumps. If you're still not sure, look at the animal's underside. The distance between the sex and anal openings is greater on males than on females. Male gerbils have dark patches of hair around their sex areas. Females don't.

HOUSE-HUNTING AND HOME CARE

Ready-Made Homes | There are a wide variety of ready-made rodent homes for sale. You can buy homes made of aluminum, glass, tin, plastic, or wire. Some are fancy, others are simple and practical. Before you buy one, think about the work involved in cleaning it. Some fancy homes are difficult to clean. And if you decide on a plastic one, be sure it has no sharp corners your pet can grab hold of and gnaw on.

Homemade Homes | If you don't want to buy a ready-made home, you can make one of your own. All you need are a few basic tools and some metal, wood, screening, or wire mesh. For hamsters, gerbils, mice, or rats, don't use cardboard or a cardboard box, because they'll quickly gnaw their way out of it. Guinea pigs don't gnaw as much as their rodent cousins, so you can house them in a large cardboard box. Replace the box when they gnaw through.

If you use wood, choose a thick plywood. You can cover the wood with screens, wire mesh, or metal to prevent gnawing. Be sure to build a large screen window or removable screen top so your pets get enough air. Tack all screening *outside* the frame.

When you're building a home, make sure you give your pets plenty of room to exercise and play. Mice, rats, hamsters, and gerbils like to stand up and climb. If you have two pets, their home should be at least one foot high, one foot wide, and two feet long. Of course, guinea pigs will need bigger homes. If you have more than two pets, build extra homes or make one extra-large home.

Absorbent and Burrowing Materials | Be sure to put in your pet's home at least an inch of absorbent and burrowing materials. Gerbils and hamsters love to dig in and out of clean sand. Mice, guinea pigs, and rats have hours of fun playing with clean wood chips, wood shavings, and sawdust. Also give your pet clean paper napkins and paper towels. It will enjoy shredding and rearranging them. All these materials will serve to absorb your pet's wastes, too.

Bedding and Nesting Materials | Rodents like to be comfortable and warm when they sleep, so give them bedding and nesting materials such as hay, straw, leaves, or fresh grass clippings. But *don't* give them any cloth. They may try to eat it.

Private Rooms and Nesting Boxes | Sometimes rodents, like people, need a little privacy to get away from it all. Give your pet small plastic, metal, or glass containers, where it can go to relax or sleep. Soup cans are fine for hamsters, mice, and gerbils. Rats don't need nesting boxes. In fact, they are easier to make friends with if they don't have nesting boxes.

Home Location | The temperature inside your pet's home should range between 65° and 80° Fahrenheit (19°

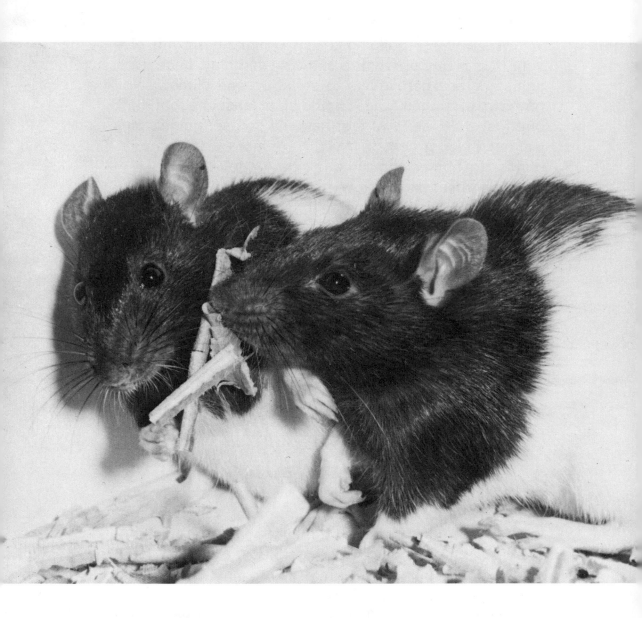

These pet rats are busy rearranging their burrowing material.
Rodents are very clean and quite fussy about keeping house.

to 26° C). Anything lower or higher can cause illness. Don't put your pet's home in a draft or in front of fans or air conditioners. Keep its home out of direct sunlight. Dogs, cats, or other animals might hurt or eat your rodent pet, so put its home out of reach from other animals, too.

House Cleaning | All you have to do to keep your pet's home clean and odor-free is to remove soiled materials and uneaten food each day, and wash the home thoroughly once a week. Don't put your pet back in its home until it is completely dry. If your hamster has hoarded food, throw away any that has spoiled, but put back the unspoiled food where you found it. Otherwise, your little friend will get very upset and will run around looking for its treasure.

Rodents usually leave their wastes in one area. You should clean out this area daily, also.

FEEDING YOUR PET

Since rodents can't shop, they have to depend on people to feed them. Your pet must be fed every day. Your pet mouse, for example, would probably die if it didn't get anything to eat for twenty-four hours. So if you're going away, make sure someone feeds it every day. Feeding rodents is easy. They are mostly vegetable eaters. You don't have to feed them meat at all.

Water | Rodents need to drink fresh water every day to stay healthy. You should have in your pet's home a gravity feed water bottle. You can buy an inexpensive one from a pet store. Fill the bottle with clean, fresh water, insert the stopper and straw, and hang the bottle, upside-down, on a wall inside your pet's home. Clean and fill the bottle with fresh water daily. Don't put bowls or dishes of water in your pet's home. The water will spill or your pet will dirty in it.

Before you choose a cage, make sure there is an easy and secure way to attach the gravity feed water bottle to it.

Gerbils don't need much water. They originally lived in the desert and thus developed the ability to "manufacture" their own water. They will probably get all the moisture they need from fruits and vegetables. But to be sure, see that water is always available to them.

Liquid multi-vitamin drops, sold at pet stores, can be added to your pet's water to insure it gets all the essential vitamins it needs.

Grains | Rodents need to eat whole grains such as barley, bran, corn, oats, soybeans, uncooked oatmeal, uncooked rice, and wheat, every day. Small pieces of fresh bread are good sources of grain. Grains contain vitamins and minerals that your pet needs to live a healthy life. Some of our rodent friends like to eat cornflakes. Others enjoy birdseed.

Vegetables | Make sure you give your pet small pieces of fresh, raw vegetables, such as carrots, clover, and spinach. One gerbil we know, Chipper, loves celery leaves. Be sure to wash all vegetables before you feed them to your pet.

Fruits | Most of the rodents we know enjoy fruits. Feed your pet small pieces of fresh apple, banana, grape, or pear every few days.

Milk | Rodents like milk, but don't give them liquid milk. It spoils too quickly. Instead, give them a teaspoon of dry milk daily.

Dry Food | Most pet stores sell a variety of packaged dry foods for rodents. All these foods provide necessary vitamins and minerals. If you feed your guinea pig dry food made for other rodents, though, be sure to add some vegetables and fruits. Guinea pigs need a lot of vitamin C.

Salt | Rodents need salt, so attach a block or spool of rock salt to the side of their home. Your pet will lick the salt whenever it feels the need.

How Much Food? | Feed your pets as much food as they want. Most rodents won't overeat. Start with one or two tablespoons of one kind of grain per meal for each pet. Always remove uneaten food, especially fruits and vegetables. They spoil quickly and can cause odors, attract insects, or make your pet sick.

When? | Feed your pet at the same time every day. Animals like regular schedules. Feeding your pet once in the morning and once in the evening is a good way to do it.

Treats | Rodents love treats (Don't we all?). You can reward your pet with raisins, peanuts, sunflower seeds, or small dog biscuits. But don't let these treats replace its regular meals.

Don'ts! | Don't feed your rodent pet cheese. It will make it fat. Don't feed your pet meat; it may make it cannibalistic. Frozen vegetables will make your pet sick, as will bruised or rotting fruits, candy, pop, or other junk foods. If you see your pet eating its waste materials, don't worry. Rodents will do this sometimes to get extra vitamins and minerals.

ENJOYING AND TRAINING YOUR PET

After you bring home your rodent pet, it may take a few days to arrange its home and get used to its new surroundings. Then it will be ready to get to know you better. If you're quiet, gentle, and patient, your furry little friend will soon learn to look forward to the time you spend with it.

Introduce Yourself | Let your little pet get to know you gradually. Slowly put your hand into its home and let it sniff you. Talk softly and gently stroke its back and the top of its head. If it runs away at first, be patient. Eventually it will come back to explore your hand. Try holding out a bit of food, and let your pet eat from your hand.

Picking Up Your Pet | Once your pet knows you, you can pick it up. Make sure you handle it carefully. Don't squeeze or jerk it, and never swoop down suddenly and grab it without warning. To pick up a hamster, gerbil, or mouse, cup your hand and scoop it up. Then hold it firmly around the middle so it doesn't fall. You should pick up a rat by putting your hand around its middle. NEVER pick up your pet by its tail. If you pick up a mouse by its tail, it will tell you how upset it is by biting or scratching you.

Always hold your gerbil gently but firmly around its middle.

You need both hands to pick up a full-grown guinea pig. Use one hand to lift the animal around the chest, then use your other hand to support its rump and hind legs. Guinea pigs are the most timid rodent pets. You can help your pet feel safe and secure by holding it close to your body.

Playtime | Rodent pets need lots of play and exercise to keep from becoming irritable and sick. They love to explore. But if you put your little friend on a table top, watch it closely to see it doesn't go too near the edge and fall off. Your pet will enjoy occasional trips on the floor. But don't leave it alone on the floor. It might gnaw at your furniture or squeeze into a spot where you can't get it out.

Pet stores have all kinds of toys for rodent pets. Rodents love playing on wheels, ladders, sliding boards, and swings. Use your imagination to make toys for them yourself. Most guinea pigs think it's a real treat to squeeze in and out of empty tissue boxes and rolls from paper towels. Mice, rats, hamsters, and gerbils all love to scurry in and out of boxes of various shapes and sizes.

Learning Tricks | To teach your rodent pet some tricks, you will need a lot of patience and a little food. Don't expect your pet to learn everything in one day, and don't shout or you will confuse and frighten it. Guinea pigs aren't very famous for learning tricks. But they will learn simple tricks if you are gentle and patient.

Daily exercise on a wheel is one of the best ways for your pet rodent to stay in shape.

Almost anything can be an adventure for a pet rodent. These
guinea pigs are having a great time crawling in and out of a cardboard
box, and their owners are having just as much fun watching them.

Start with a simple command. Hold out a treat and say "Come." When your pet comes to the food, let it nibble. Then move your hand away, hold out some more food, and say "Come" again. Use the food as a reward. Give it only when your pet obeys you. If you repeat the exercise enough, your pet will learn to come even if you don't give it food.

Practice with your pet at the same time each day, and always use the same command. Don't work at it for more than thirty minutes at a time. And don't be discouraged if your gerbil would rather look around than listen to you. Gerbils are especially curious. They just don't have long attention spans. Your gerbil will be more ready to learn if it hasn't had any food for one hour before the training session.

With patience, you can teach your pets to stand on their hind legs, climb up your arm, and do other tricks. A few fourth-graders taught Willy, their pet rat, to run up their arms and perch on their shoulders. Some people have even trained mice to perform in a mouse circus.

HEALTH CARE

Rodent pets are hardy and healthy little animals. They don't get sick easily and can't give people any of their diseases. To keep your pet healthy, provide a balanced diet every day and clean its home once a week. Also, anyone with a cold should keep away from your rodent pet, especially if your pet is a hamster. A person with a cold can infect a rodent.

Runny Noses and Sniffles | If your pet does catch a cold, put the animal somewhere safe while you clean its home. Thoroughly wash the entire home, including water bottles, food containers, and toys, with soap and hot water. Replace all absorbent, bedding, and nesting materials with clean, fresh, dry materials. Don't return your pet until its home is completely dry. Then move the home to a warm, dry area, and cover it with cloth or paper to keep out drafts.

Coughing, Wheezing, and Heavy Breathing | Your pet's home is probably damp or wet, or it's in a draft. Check for spilled water or move the home.

Diarrhea | If your pet leaves loose, wet droppings, it is suffering from diarrhea. An unbalanced diet, especially too many fruits and vegetables, is the most common cause of diarrhea. Stale, rotten, or unwashed foods can also cause diarrhea.

Stop feeding your pet fruits and vegetables for one to three days, or until its droppings look normal. You aren't feeding your rodent enough fruits and vegetables if it leaves hard, dry droppings.

Blood | If you see blood in your pet's waste materials, you're probably not feeding it a balanced diet or enough food.

Dull Fur | You aren't feeding your pet enough grains or dried milk if its fur gets dull or ruffled. Be sure you feed it at least one tablespoon of grain and one teaspoon of dried milk every day.

Inflamed Organs | If your pet develops red, raw areas around its sex organs, you aren't giving it enough clean, fresh water. The problem should clear up in a few days, when the animal has drunk enough fresh water.

Sores | If you see raw and red areas or sores around your pet's mouth and nose, your little friend has probably been burrowing and rubbing too hard. These should heal by themselves in a few days. If they don't, wash the area gently with warm water. If the sores still don't heal, apply a mild antiseptic, such as mercurochrome or tincture of iodine. To help prevent these sores, be sure all parts of your pet's home are smooth. No nails, staples, screws, or splinters should stick out.

Hair Loss | Rodents sometimes lose hair when they rub against parts of their home to scratch. Other times, in fighting with each other, hair gets pulled out. Don't worry, the hair will grow back. By the way, if your pets fight a lot, they may be telling you they need a larger home. If they continue to fight in a larger home, you will have to give them separate homes.

Cage Paralysis | This is most likely caused by a vitamin D deficiency. The symptoms are difficulty in moving, poor appetite, and a run-down look. Bread dipped in cod liver oil can quickly relieve the problem.

Quarantine | If you have a sick pet, put it alone in a temporary home. Otherwise, your healthy pets may get sick too. Feed the sick rodent bread dipped in warm milk, and let it alone.

Call the Vet | You should call a veterinarian if your pet won't stop bleeding, has been sick for more than five days, or has a problem you can't identify or aren't sure how to treat.

Death | Rodents don't live very long lives compared to people. Keep this in mind before you decide on what kind of pet to choose. It is never easy to lose a pet you have grown fond of.

When your rodent pet dies, remove it from its home right away and dispose of it outside. If your pet died from a disease, clean the cage and have a parent soak it in boiling water before you put another animal in it. Otherwise, your new pet may catch the disease.

FAMILY PLANNING

It's easy to start a rodent family. Adult males and females will usually mate without any encouragement from you. If you have more than one female guinea pig, mouse, or rat living with a male, the male will probably mate with all the females. WATCH OUT: you could have a population explosion! Gerbils choose one mate for life. Even if her "husband" dies, a gerbil "widow" will probably not accept a new mate. Hamsters are discussed below.

Most rodents can have babies before their bodies are ready. A mother who gives birth too early might not be strong enough to bear and take care of her babies. So you should keep your adult males and females in separate homes until it's safe for them to mate. (See chart on page 54.)

Male rodents are ready to mate at any time. Females have an *estrus cycle* that makes them fertile and ready to mate only at certain times. For example, a female gerbil's cycle is four to six days. During each cycle, eggs form and develop in the female's body. The eggs are ready for the male to fertilize on only one day. When fertilization occurs, the female becomes pregnant. The estrus cycle

BREEDING AND GROWTH INFORMATION

	GERBIL	GUINEA PIG	HAMSTER	MOUSE	RAT
ABLE TO MATE AT	10–12 weeks	4 weeks	4 weeks	4–6 weeks	11–12 weeks
EARLIEST RECOMMENDED MATING AGE	10–12 weeks	16–24 weeks	8 weeks	8–12 weeks	14–15 weeks
ESTRUS CYCLE	4–6 days	12–18 days	4 days	4–5 days	5 days
LENGTH OF PREGNANCY	24–25 days	65–70 days	16 days	19–21 days	18–21 days
NUMBER IN LITTER	1–12 Average: 5	1–6 Average: 2–3	1–15 Average: 7	2–12 Average: 5	1–17 Average: 9
WHEN BABIES' EYES OPEN	20 days	At birth	14–15 days	12–13 days	10–12 days
WEANING AGE	21–35 days	10–14 days	20–24 days	21–28 days	14–21 days
MATURE LENGTH	4 inches, not counting tail	9–10 inches	6 inches	2½–3½ inches, not counting tail	7–8 inches, not counting tail
MATURE WEIGHT	3 ounces	32 ounces	3–4 ounces	½–1 ounce	8–14 ounces
LIFE SPAN	3–4 years	5–7 years	2 years	2 years	3 years

repeats itself continually, so your pets have many chances to mate and produce babies during their lifetime.

Hamster Courtship | The female hamster is fussier than other rodents about mating. She has to be introduced to her mate slowly. Sometimes she will reject him. You have to be patient and hope for the best. NEVER put the male in the female's home when she's in it. The female may fight or even kill him. First, put the male in the female's home while you put the female in the male's home. This will give both hamsters a chance to get used to each other's smells. After a while, return the hamsters to their own homes. Put the homes side by side, so your pets can become friendly. If the hamsters seem friendly, put them together in the male's home one evening. The female will probably start a fight if she's not ready to mate. You should then separate them, and try again the next night. Even if they don't mate right away, it's safe to leave them together for a few days, up to a week, as long as they are not fighting.

Caring for Your Pregnant Female | You can tell that your female rodent is pregnant when she has an enlarged abdomen. You may be able to see ripples or bulges on her sides from the babies growing inside her. When you know your pet is pregnant, carefully move her to her own clean home, so she can rest in peace and quiet. Don't handle her after the move, because you may injure the babies. If you just have one pair of gerbils or rats, it's all right to leave them together. To prevent disturbances, clean the cage right after mating. Then you don't have to bother the female during her pregnancy.

Your pet will probably want a little box and lots of nesting materials, such as clean paper towels, hay, or straw, so she can build a nest for her babies. During her pregnancy, give her extra food, plenty of milk, and all the water she wants.

Birth | If you see your pet giving birth, be careful not to disturb her. You can watch the birth if you're quiet. Don't move around, and don't shine any lights into the home. Even if the mother seems to be having problems, leave her alone. If you upset her during birth, she may not care for her babies properly. She may even eat them.

Gerbil, hamster, mouse, and rat babies are born without hair and with their eyes closed. Newborn guinea pigs look like miniature adults. Their eyes are open, they have teeth, and they have a full coat of fur. They usually get up and start running around a few minutes after they're born.

Care After Birth | When the birth is completed, look into the nest and remove any babies that were born dead. But be careful not to touch the mother or her live babies. If she smells your scent on her children, she may neglect them. If you must touch any of the babies in an emergency, first rub your hands in the bedding. This will mask your scent. Also, touch *all* the babies so they all will smell the same. If one of the babies smells different from the others, the mother will think it is a stranger and she may kill it or her whole litter. Leave the family alone for a few days. The mother will clean and nurse her children. Be sure she has plenty of food, milk, and water.

When you see the babies begin to nibble on their mother's food, be sure to add extra. You can begin wean-

Golden hamsters at one day, one week, and three weeks old.

ing the babies by feeding them bread soaked in milk. By the time the new family is completely weaned, you should be able to tell the males from the females. It's a good idea to put the sexes in separate homes then, so they don't mate too early.

The Father's Role | Most rodent fathers don't do very much to help with the children. In fact, if a mouse father is there when his children are born, he may eat them. Rats are better fathers. But a mother rat probably won't let her mate near the children for a few days. After that, he helps to keep the babies warm. Gerbil fathers take even more of an interest in their families. They wash the babies, keep them warm, play with them, and help rearrange the nest.

LOVING AND RESPECTING

Throughout his life, Papa, our grandfather, taught us to love and respect all animals. He never wanted any animal to suffer or be mistreated by human hands. We can remember many times when Papa reminded us of our responsibilities to animals.

Your rodent pets depend on you. If these little animals lived in their natural environments, they would take care of themselves. But your pets really need your love and respect to survive.

Before you put a mature female and male in the same home, be sure you're prepared to take care of the babies when they are born. You will need more housing space and will have to supply more food. If you aren't prepared for more pets, give them to a responsible friend or pet store.

Don't set your pets free in fields, prairies, vacant lots, or forests. They probably won't survive. Very likely, they will be eaten by other animals or die from the cold.

Remember, rodents want to be friendly and have friends. They want to love and be loved. They will surely respect you if you respect them.

Rodents don't live long lives. So it's up to you to make their short lives happy and healthy.

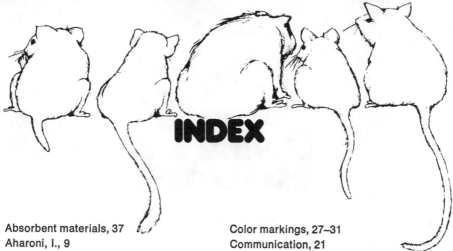

INDEX

ABOUT THE AUTHORS

James and Lynn Hahn are the authors of *Recycling: Re-using our World's Solid Wastes; Plastics* (a First Book); *The Metric System* (a First Book); and *Environmental Careers* (a Career Concise Guide), all published by Franklin Watts. Currently, they are working on books, articles, poems, and stories about other animals and how they live in our changing environment.

We sincerely appreciate the cooperation of Irene Roetter at Roetter's Shasta Pet Center, Glenview, Illinois, and Fluffy, the Peruvian guinea pig, Romeo and Juliet, the long-haired hamsters, and all of our other rodent friends. Special thanks to Robert H. Geisler, G. Gould, James S. Mello, B. Wall, and to Robbie and David Estok—and Chipper, their gerbil.

Photos courtesy of:
The Charles River Companies, frontispiece, pp. 3 (lower), 10 (upper); World Health Organization, p. 3 (upper); New York Public Library Picture Collection, p. 4 (upper); Adam and Charles Black Publishers, p. 4 (lower); New York Zoological Society, pp. 7, 10 (lower); Blue Spruce Farms, pp. 13, 19, 30, 38; Pfizer, Inc., pp. 20, 24; Oasis Pet Products, pp. 22, 41; Engle Laboratory Animals, Inc., pp. 34, 57; James Sage Hahn and Lynn Lowery Hahn, pp. 29, 45, 47, 48.

Cover design by Beehive Design Studio, Inc.